The Tyrant of the Past and the Slave of the Future

The Tyrant of the Past and the Slave of the Future

Christopher Davis

Texas Tech University Press
1989

This book was set in 10 on 13 Baskerville and printed on acid-free paper that meets the guidelines for permanence and durability of the Committee on Production Guidelines for Book Longevity of the Council on Library Resources. ∞

Jacket and book design by Joanna Hill
Cover art by Steve Ogelsby

Printed in the United States of America

Library of Congress Cataloging-in-Publication Data

Davis, Christopher, 1960–
    The tyrant of the past and the slave of the future.

    I. Title.
PS3554.A9334T9   1989   811'.54   89-4996
ISBN 0-89672-199-X (alk. paper)
ISBN 0-89672-200-7 (pbk. alk. paper)

Texas Tech University Press
Lubbock, Texas 79409-1037 USA

To Ben, my brother
(August 6, 1963–May 1, 1979)
and to my parents

Acknowledgments

My thanks to the editors of the following journals, in which these poems first appeared:

Agni Review: "To Amelia Earhart"

The American Poetry Review: "Jojo's," "My Grandmother's Manifest Destiny," "Jack Frost's Question," "In This Blackout," "Clarence White Escapes His Demon Lover," "The Sacrifices"

Boston Review: "Lust," "The Angels of Earth"

Chicago Review: "The Murderer"

Crazyhorse: "(Unfinished Poem about Mary Queen of Scots)," "Taps"

Denver Quarterly: "The Only Pasture We Can Graze in," "His Prayer," "Clarence White's Angel is a Witch," "Song about a Meadow in Sunset"

Ironwood: "O I Am Very Sick and Sorrowful," "World War Three"

North American Review: "Look at the Obese Loser Trying Not to Pray"

Pavement: "Envoi Written at a Coffeeshop Window"

Sonora Review: "Clarence White Exposed by High Noon," "Clarence White Seduced by an Icecube"

James White Review: "If We Can't Surrender Greed to Love We'll Murder Earth"

For her unending faith, encouragement, and friendship, I would like to thank Jorie Graham. Thanks and love to Steve.

Foreword

Gauguin said, when it suddenly became a great discovery to him, "I now believe that all great art is exaggeration," and I believe he said, as part of the same thought, that salvation lies in extremes. This brings to mind immediately Blake's "palace of wisdom," which was itself an angry, or desperate, response to Greek and continental admonitions of moderation and symmetry. I think it is in this light that Chris Davis's poetry must be perceived. It is a poetry of exaggeration and extremes, just as it is a poetry of excess, a word dear to the heart of Blake and hideous (he thought) to his enemies. I am struck by the fact that much of the great music and poetry and painting of the last two hundred years is not only excessive, in the wonderful sense of that word, but was rejected and laughed at—hated—just because of those excesses. What is amazing is how quickly the exaggerated art became acceptable—and valuable. Ginsberg's *Howl* was ridiculed in 1957, but was taught in conservative universities only four or five years later, probably by some of the same people who did the ridiculing. It took Gauguin himself only a few years longer for his paintings to be praised and treasured.

Davis's excesses and exaggerations are unmistakable and consistent. They consist—from a negative point of view—of his abandoning traditional (nonpoetic) logic, sentence structure, and punctuation. But from the opposing, and complementary, point of view, they consist—I almost want to add "merely"—of deeply passionate speech and of incredibly juxtaposed utterances that overwhelm the reader as they tumble forth in a dazzling and shameless barrage—that overwhelm the reader because they amaze him and embarrass and even puzzle him in their directness and nakedness. I sometimes think that truly original poetry is the result of new language, and I sometimes think that it is the result of new ideas and subjects, or originally conceived ones. But maybe it's the result of something lucidly or unequivocally *felt* and, as a result of that feeling, both the language and the subject matter appear, or really become, original. If this is true, then it is the lucid and unequivocal feeling that is radical and original, although for some poets the word *posture* or *point of view* or *position* or even *vision* would be more appropriate than the word *feeling*. I think this is true for Wordsworth and Auden and Ashbery and James Wright. It is true also for Villon, and

Burns. On the one hand, it seems as if an entirely new language or vocabulary or even grammar were being given to us; on the other hand, what is given seems absolutely familiar, even obvious. Other poets, all of whom are given to deep admiration (which poses as envy) will say—in every case—"Why didn't I think of that?" In this case, they would mean, "Why didn't I have that lucidity, that unequivocal feeling?"

In "Look at the Obese Loser Trying Not to Pray," there is an unrelenting mixture of anger and fear and nostalgia that makes the reader almost flinch with pain and pity. The references (in the form of vivid images) are obscure in their privacy, the line of reasoning is fragmented and disorderly, and the sentences run into each other; but the unity is overwhelming, the passion is singular, final, and vividly centered, the language is ecstatic, the vision is unique—and deadly. My temptation is to move into biography and psychoanalysis. Davis did have a brother named Ben, and that brother was murdered, and there is no question that that death has haunted Chris Davis and entered into poem after poem; but it is the art I am interested in and the structure of the poem—the created agony. And I am interested in the means that he uses to create that agony, and I am interested in the heroic and moral clarity, the "lucid and unequivocal feeling" that makes that agony possible.

Look at the Obese Loser Trying Not to Pray
to my dead brother

You faraway Holy
Ghost filling my skull don't You remember
the widow next door She failed to censor
off her drunken pool's scum breeding
mosquitoes Why did our mother and father try
evicting her? I could have
loved her We heard
from her shadowy kitchen sizzling
pork-smells Did she choke her body free in there Me
    stretched out flat
skull raped by soap-smells on the
laundry-room's hard carpet
the weak floor trembling at the washing-
machine's rumbling maybe all
she'd felt dissolved into her

home The dawn after
I'd shoved You off my treehouse breaking open Your
      head to free
her ghost I keep
evicting back through shadows we slunk
out to our private
burned-down chickencoop to scribble
on its charred puddles of rain her name *Christopher* in
piss Why did You
tell me she'll feel trapped until "death" takes me? Ben
I came home early from Your tear-stupid funeral I crept
back inside
our living-room's cold cave I
curled I twitched like a larva born on mental scum on its
lake-bottom deep blue and
in the carpet found a hole
where the vacuum-cleaner's pink seemingly
endless missing hose should fit I
opened the silver trap I prayed
You'd feel these wants like
any brother should You'd
switch on the groaning central system from our
basement You'd suck
my skull safe into this warm house make the
two of us one ghost Please let
my nerves be home's
"immutable" wires
A door slams Please
seem someone real at last Don't
let Ben take me

    The artifacts of our culture are there—a central vacuum system, the swimming pool, the carpeted laundry room—it could be any suburban home, or even one of those exurban or slightly rural ones, for there is a tree house and a former chicken coop, but what counts is not those things as such—it is hardly worth mentioning them—but the emotion, that is, the *mind* of the poet as he lives through those things, and turns them into symbols, and sees them as either significant events, or stations, or desperate points of reference—orientation—on his slide into hell, or understanding. And though the reader can create a narrative, or a drama, there is always an unknown (I prefer that to private) reference—(the widow, the "'immutable' wires")—which, in the case of Davis's poetry, provides pleasure, the kind derived from mystery, rather than confusion. Poem after poem is like this.

As far as influence, I see the New York poets, particularly Ashbery, Ginsberg of *Kaddish*, Zbigniew Herbert, Kafka, maybe Gil Orlovitz, if Davis has ever read him. What is maybe a little more interesting than influences is models, prototypes, predecessors. I think Davis is in the line of Shelley—Rimbaud—Hart Crane. Although it's not the "thorns of life" that he bleeds upon—he is not a black bird hanging on a tree of nails—it's more a bomb left over from the Boer War, a crazy accident, and he's less a bird than a kind of heavy groundhog, or mole. I think of Hart Crane in particular, though I don't know altogether why. Maybe it's the ruptured and lovely language; maybe it's the direct encounter with the demonic. May I suggest that certain of Davis's poems, "Lust," for example, or "O I Am Very Sick and Sorrowful," "My Grandmother's Manifest Destiny," "At an Intersection"—a dozen others, of course, are superb. He has a voice that is altogether his own; he has great courage; a magic instinct, a deeply felt subject. It's a wonderful book.

—Gerald Stern

Contents

Three

The Sacrifices

Lust

Pressed in, pressed down by books:
hasn't read them and can't. Can't talk
for kissing their spines. Why write
with a half-ton of pages
packed for donation to a charity?
Can't even lift the boxes. Only one
jacaranda looms over him,
unrolling its shadow onto the page—
he's nobody else, he'd like you to be,
wishes he could cheat God, seduce you
into wanting yourself—heavy
boy like him on fat earth.

The Invisible Snake

Jojo's

The night my brother was stabbed,
but not quite stabbed to death,
I was drinking wine in a coffeeshop
called Jojo's with some friends.
He'd been walking home drunk
from a party. Two guys who'd shared a case
of beer had picked him up.
After stabbing him, they threw him
down into a canyon. Parasites
kept his wounds clean: two days later,
he climbed out. He was
found at the side of the road by
two guys. He would not let them
touch him. On May 1st,
he died in the hospital.

I've forgotten if I had a good time that night
with my friends. I probably did.
We were all in a band together.
A month later, I
left that town to go to college.
The rest of them moved too, I think.
No: on a trip home at Christmas
I saw Nancy at Jojo's. (They had
found my phone number in his pocket.)
I don't know what
was said, if we did talk.

To Amelia Earhart

The inside of most clouds is clammy grey, wet and
forbidding.

Walking through the USC medical school with
my brother, I
saw a monkey strapped
to a board: the
skin on its skull was pulled
back, the denuded
brain fixed with wires.
A one-way window kept
us out of the lab. I believe it's
our right, to
fly too far
into a thought. The monkey's
eyes, taped open, stared with-
out motion at a pulsing
beam of lamplight. Years
later, standing
next to my brother on his
deathbed, I
could not look directly at
his body. In the
electroencephalograph's screen, a slow
green electrical snake pulsed
—describing what?—and I stood
in the sterile room, thinking.
It began to pulse slower, then it
lay down heavily
to sleep. Break
the window. Turn the
lights on. Don't leave me
alone. I can feel
my own thought here.

The Invisible Man

There were two souls inside him,
one his and one his dead brother's,
each withheld from the other
though they drifted without shape of thought
or perception
through his one body's corridors.

Nearing the stained-glass pattern his eyes cast
on the opposite wall of his mind,
one soul would cry out to its counterpart
as though rays of the warm world were themselves
a kind of danger:

they were: to him, change was a weapon.
But cartons of old photographs were left
unopened in the next room.
It was the power of conflict,
the uncertainty, the cold crying-out
of each soul which moved them
as close together in this life as possible.

The Only Pasture We Can Graze in

A January night. Calmer
and no more resistant than death,
chaos frozen into forms, not patterns,
the park across the street
feels nothing for the fog moving through it
slowly, as if fog walked in a sleep, refuses
to let the fog nestle in its snow
and the cold central lamp can't
steam the snow up
from the suicidal grass.
A boy walking toward me in a red coat,
his face as pale as the fog, his hair
not glittering, black like the sky.
The swing he walks past doesn't
swing, hanging on chains that never squeak,
he doesn't seem to see it
or care, and behind him
the little toy fort of black pine
doesn't ask him to turn
come in
let go of the three blind mice nipping his eyes.
I want to live. Here he comes,
I don't want to know his name yet
or tame him, he isn't a knife
coming at me from behind.
Forehead pressed on cold glass,
I put my forearm between glass
and head. Keep
walking. You can eat me
like the sun touching grass, but slowly,
let me live for three months.

My Grandmother's Manifest Destiny

She could not be the mongoose she saw
in Barbados.
Old coffeestains covered her beige dress: I'd
like to believe she brought
Paradise with her. "It looks just like
one of my squirrels back home,"

she insulted the tourguide. His job
was to smile and say, "These were transplanted
from India."

The mongoose had leapt from
tall weeds. Crossed
the road and
disappeared.
Into other tall weeds. It
had not bared its teeth to her:
as she shed no whole skins,
she could not be
a snake.

A jet's moan swallowed whatever
she said next. She pushed
her gold wedding band up
to her knuckle,
then back. Like hers,
is my world still a
map of my innocence?
Her husband had just died.
I wanted to go home.

That afternoon, getting out of the taxi, I stepped
on a live snail. It
happened to be there.
My mind oozed into
its shell, and
that moment was my home.

Jack Frost's Question

for R.S.

Nine ducks waiting for the river to thaw
squawking on the snow-covered ice
breadcrumbs on a white plate a hundred years across my
    kitchen
how could they pass up our feed to fly south
simply staring at them now I'd get nowhere I might get
    out of my arrangements
I'm half-drowning under ice anyway help
me don't watch my cold lips tell this story
when the sun staggers staining the ice red that stiletto
    called the moon takes its light you
know duck's blood was once
used in relics in the days when penetration could be
    bought
a crystal tube which for a coin the priest would warm in
    his fist under the table
do your lovers remind you of dead lovers
do you fear cameras
it's like an instinct thinking aloud it's no one's fault
smudges I can't wash from my hands squawking
ducks deaf ducks there's
no justice
if I could drown your summons in my blood or
drown my blood wouldn't I still be a widowed
shooting gallery target to the fuckers in those cars
    crossing the bridge?

6

The Invisible Snake

They once wrapped a
fed boa around my shoulders

and my torso: its arrowhead
head with the red, to me

occasional tongue rubbed my
jaw: the other end

where it tapered to
whip-width was wrapped

high up around my thigh. Its cold
heft felt like

armor. It was heavy and smooth.
Its muscles expanded and

returned as it crept
over my skeleton, maybe to feel it, maybe

rehearsing to take me
to that, maybe to keep from

sliding down. Weakened
down to the earth, pressed

into myself
by this tunnel of muscle

a calm overpowered
me. The snake

was taken off. They
gave it to the body of

another, some betrayer, some
fig-shape, a soon-to-be-fearing

feared shadow far away.

7

(Unfinished Poem about Mary Queen of Scots)

1.
It occurs to me now
that if Mary Stuart were to understand
exactly how we are trapped,
we would not be able to picture her
wearing the black and white clothing
for which, in her day,
she was known. "La reine blanche"
is what the French called her,
making no use of opposites.
The French were ahead of their time.
I think she wore it at first
because to mourn was appropriate,
and the Scots took it seriously;
but when, a year after
her first husband's death,
her court went into half-mourning,
she did not follow suit.
No doubt it had been a long year.
Reports, no doubt,
of what John Knox was saying
(that she'd danced after midnight
at the slaughter of Heugonots)
had done little to welcome her.
She did not stop officially mourning
for another five years,
when she married Lord Darnley—
but by that time, I think,
black and white were her colors.

2.
Where are the symbols
for an easier life? I've changed,
I am changing, the leaves
on my neighbor's front lawn
are of so many reds now
they're the reds in my memory.
Impossible now not to think
of my brother, and the dried blood

8

I saw in his hair: the hair
and the blood were both red.
So was Mary's. In my end
is my Beginning. Should I hate
the two people who killed him?
I can't. It has nothing to do
with forgiveness: a matter of self-
preservation, perhaps, or else some
ambiguous guilt—as if I
killed him! There is no Elizabeth.
It seems as if no one force
is at fault, not even "society."
But it happened, his murder,
I know that: it happened so quickly
and without cause or warning
it seems to have reached out
from nowhere to take him, a rope
tossed out a train window.
Where is objectivity? It happened:
but where, and to whom?

The Angels of Earth

An afternoon soaked with rain. Far off
a stroke of thunder.
Across the street, on the lawn, in a tent
of clear plastic, four plumbers kneel in yellow raincoats.
The dark brick church they're reviving
stands behind them.
They use torches. Probably welding
a new joint onto an old pipe
four or five feet down
in the soil. At the moment
they probably want to stay dry, to be paid,
go inside for a late lunch, maybe
find an arrowhead or bones.
A blue flame fills their masks.

My father hides in an evergreen bush.
He hugs the corkscrew trunk
as if for warmth; he clenches it
between his thighs, legs crossed like thick roots above
    ground.
Should he ask those plumbers
for his father, whom he never met?
Or for his unmet mother? Should he ask
for the bed he was born in?
A raindrop falls from his nose
to his lap. He takes off his steamy glasses.
In the curb, a drain gulps the small river
that can't turn the tires of a parked
empty hearse. All the secrets,
all his questions can't be God.

A Brazilian

There are rooms in which one lie will save your life.

His mattress has been heaved end-up
against the wall: he's a
naked, brown curl on the floor
at its foot. White
Bufferin scattered hopelessly among the splinters of
    glass around
his head.
A red blanket spilling
in over the windowsill.
I heard the tinkle of a breaking window
from my apartment upstairs: I looked
out and saw a pillow on the gray snow.
His delicate face seems
Oriental. His eyes are closed tightly and
he's giggling.
One hand is lost from sight between his thighs;
the other arm is stretched toward us across the floor, the
    fingers open, the palm shown.

Elaine and I are in the doorway, afraid
to go in, afraid of his epileptic seizure
or of his madness, afraid to
talk, afraid to touch him.

That red blanket—broken
jaw in a beautiful face.

Then a paramedic and a cop kneeling over
him, the paramedic
shaking his shoulders till his eyes open, the eyes
    bloodshot
and vivid, moving
quickly over all of us.
Come on, the cop says. He tries to half-roll, half-
    sidewind away from
their hands. Together
they brace down his shoulders and his ankles.

I stand
trembling and there's
nothing I can do.
Come on son.
His eyelids
close; the pupils swim hungrily back to
their depths.

He can't kick his body loose. He
chokes air in and
sobs it out.

Portugee. Portugee. Portugee. Portugee.

The Untamed World

The richest lagoons in the world
are paused now between
the Barrier Reef and the Australian mainland.
More crustaceans live in these waters
and abandon their shells underneath
coral branches
than in any other waters in the world.
These facts are my body.
The crown-of-thorns starfish, once
checked by the Triton—whose shell
makes too good a souvenir
on the mainland—eats coral, thus
"turning the reefs into an under-water wasteland."
    Marine life's
most active at night here. The face
of this world confronts us with history. My friend
has the flu, and last night
we stayed at home, watching TV.
Late, late at night, his eyes
seemed to swim to the surface of his glasses,
asking—but what was the question?
I had not thought of leaving. Had he?
In the mirror now: what was the question?

The Two Seasons

A Spring morning. Soon
a haze will arrive
it will thicken the sun and the air
will be heat-clogged and moist
like air in an igloo: now
the dust
glitters as it falls, each mote seduced
a few steps down the road's shoulder
by the breeze. God
slams the door of his pickup. He
climbs over the barbed-wire fence. Out here in the high
   grass
he folds his coat over his arm
wipes his glasses with Kleenex
begins:

In this meadow I dreamed last night, it's still evening.
   Crickets sing all around me in the grass. A brook
   chatters somewhere . . . in front of those four white-
   petalled dogwood at the far edge—standing so close
   together and in full flower, their tops make one top,
   but there are four trunks—the tips of reeds stick up
   from a ditch. In thirty years, that's where the main
   elevator's lobby door will slide open. I'll bet I could
   smell those petals if the breeze would turn this way.
   Behind the dogwood, on the horizon, the sun makes a
   long, orange curve, like the ass of a woman. A fifth
   dogwood, charred black and splintered by lightning,
   stands a few yards east of the others. Death is no
   crime. I think of its petals and feel nothing. A crooked
   limb sticks out, too thick for the breeze to snap off, as
   if reaching for the woman in the wrong place. A crow
   from behind me sails down into the grass, a falling
   shadow in the twilight. The woman has turned away

completely. On a far hill, between the horizon and the dogwood, at the center of dusk, a radio tower's red light pulses. Off and on. Off and on. Off. On

a Spring night
in the cab of his pickup
God lights a cigarette

flinches when your high beams fill his rearview
mirror

The Angels of Earth

The Murderer

As I talked, I kept thinking,
You're only guilty if they
can find it: but they'd fixed pads
to my temples and wrists. Now
I want to tell them something.
Last night, in a dream,
I watched a crusted gray whale
dying underwater, the bad end
of a steel harpoon
broken off in its side.
It was going down slowly,
horizontal, turning over
on its back, on its belly,
the blood weaving out
and wrapping around its whole length
like a frayed blanket. Then it
broke through a school of thousands
of tiny silver fish
and disappeared.
I guess it hit bottom. The blanket
kept unraveling up from the shadows,
staining all the water, all
the fish, and even the filtered
weak columns of sunlight.
I woke, and lay half an hour
on my iron bed.
I hardly know what I've done.

The Underground Parking-Lot Night Attendant's Camouflage

My fingers stay as cold
as the concrete wall it hurt
me this evening to touch. Loving life
is letting attitudes,
not principles, count
and the best man tries to make life better
for us all? That's not
possible, survival means
nobody is good. Here I sit,
surrounded by glass,
Exhibit Z, your last human,
pressing my neck across cold window-grooves
to watch you drive down into what
to my helpless eye is darker
and more piss-stained than I'll let my heart be
though on the monitor screen I see all—
your lips moving to let words die
in echoes,
their own echoes, and cold cars
lined up like mute pigs. Once
I watched a girl getting raped
down there. I called the cops. No squad car ever came.
How are you, ma'am? Fine, how are you? Your
     headlights,
lady, didn't blind me, spread
the shadow of this booth across gray rock. Here's your
     ticket, ma'am.
Why thank you! Oh, excuse me, ma'am, I dropped my
     lighter. There it is,
I'll get it. Thank you, ma'am.
My, it's a nice one,
what a nice shade of green. Ma'am, I want to spread
     your brains
across the floor, spin
that car around and drive past
this hollow booth, drive out
into summer and night, where water
splashes in a fountain, filtered water, white water
turned blue by blue tiles. Baby

come back, I'll save your life, I heard you thinking it,
what I thought. You're cold down there,
aren't you? If like your radio I sang out
would you drive back up?
Turn off your radio? Sit on my lap?

O I Am Very Sick and Sorrowful

Can't they hear me?
                                        As always, I abandoned
my bed to hunt daylight, that chill killer
—I shall never
go back. One nickel and two pennies
in my pocket, and me
in the dawn's fog hungry . . .
each pair of small eyes drew me into its head
without question, almost
fed me there, and winked me into a rumpled, warm
    bed . . .
I marched among them unreproved onto their
    playground.
He with the Boy Scout knife twirling down
from his fingers, I thought he might like to come at me,
stab it into me slowly
for that rape he'd seen
(he must have seen) the real me performing on his ghost
behind my back
—why?—him perpetually
pegging the blade into the grass,
spurring the
dead, the true dead, O if only
to wake them back to life
and so free him. Precisely
how I picture it occurring
—will you blame me?—
the knife slips from his aim, and stabs
out all her tears and her eye-blood
onto the green, wrinkled skirt hiding the teacher,
her whistle still shrieking in her lips.
                                        Can

this host of dead children in me weep
with her?

Scissors Gleaming in Lamplight

All that summer
the chemical laboratory stayed
locked. A tube of yellow plastic hung
from its second-story window: underneath that
sat a trashbin
filled with broken wood, bits of plaster
and red wire. Once
a redbird flew off with some wire.
A sign on the door said
CLOSED FOR RENOVATION. Newspaper covered
the windows. I never
heard hammers inside. Nothing
else came down through
that tube. Maybe the guts
were all on the outside already.

Each morning
I sat across the street, waiting
for a bus I
never suspected could be on time:
the day it came
it found me half-naked, head
back, my eyes shut, talking
only to the toddler I'd roped
to my beltloop, feeling
heat on my face and not naming it
—reaching into
my pocket for scissors
and a quarter—
not yet understanding
heaven and hell are the same place.

World War Three

Trying to
feed pigeons popcorn in a neat park boundaried
by Chicago and Michigan Avenues we
watch an old man wearing a tux
dig in the dirt around
a toothlike hunk of marble The sign on it
honors "the men who sacrificed
their lives in World War One"
Around the monument's a wreath
of painted blue pinecones
Also grass
A gold caterpillar crawls from between the man's shoes

He has a white bag
in one hand in the other a trowel
Maybe he once lost a contact-lens
No seed no fertilizer comes from the bag Nothing
goes into the bag All the bones
rotted elsewhere
the teeth bite tree-roots in France
under those words isn't
much maybe seeds

Cars honk at the intersection smell them
A young man and woman walk past
they sound like a catfight See
that glass skyscraper reflects us
we're those two bright blobs by the bench don't
we live there

Listen see
where he is now stand there when he's gone
take off your glasses be quiet
in the hot sun stand still like a cornstalk
let me see you alive
once click your tongue against your teeth
aim your eyes woo the pigeons

Envoi Written at a Coffeeshop Window

On the frozen rain, I made my flat
soles shuffle and be nimble. O

postman crossing the street against
the light that

cuts the worm Traffic into pieces
we can look at, you too

must watch your feet now. If
someday you collect this small

flipbook of dancesteps, don't
take it moist-eyed down a dry

rural route: the ogress Nature might
tuck it in the bosom

of her red and green gown. Who'd
know we were buried in fire

and grass? The smoke-
gray pigeons on those distant antennae won't

sing to each other old
songs of what the early bird catches

once we're caught.

At an Intersection

From his limousine
the tyrant guessed into the
eyes of a laundry woman
and wept not for what he could not be
but less,
all he'd promised he would be.
The next morning all the blood was washed
out of his bathtub.
Now few remember him.
No one remembers the laundry woman
who crossed the street and went
home to live a little more easily, though in the end the
    same
upholstery killed her. I remember
finding a skeletal piglet out-
side a pigpen on a hot day; grass
was knitting the bones into the sun.
Flies singing
everywhere, sparrows in the grass,
cool mud-stink from the barn
and the stare of the grunting black boar we called our
    king.
That's how it feels where our ribs touch.
I will never put my hand over my eyes.
I'll keep loving all I'm given to
love, there's no other revenge.

Taps

The TV plays without its sound. The news is
from the bedroom—
the sound of your breath
as you sleep.
Like those construction men across the street
daily tapping nail after
nail into boards,
building a house for someone else, we
built love to keep our-
selves hid from ourselves,
the way milk in a glass hides the glass—
though we have a glass painted with a winter scene
in which milk becomes snow.
Now, drinking rich coffee from a mug with
my name on it, you
turn the sound up to hear the news . . .
I go into the bedroom.
Trust makes me shiver: I
trust I'll keep doubting you won't die.
Lying on this warm bed, almost
wearing the body you wear, your laughter taps
me on the back
of my head. Real
shivers, outside, would
be worse: wind hits the loose
pane of the window like a branch that isn't
there.

Christmas Eve

Up on stage, stuck at the pine's tip, a silver globe
the size of God's heart reflects the us,
erasing each solitary face. Red
sweatshirts blur all over it
like wounds. Dear father I can't
say what you feel but am I faking
the words of this shared hymn,
me standing next to my boyfriend,
your boyfriend standing next to you, my true
voice rhyming only with feedback
from the mike held away from the lips
of the big-breasted songleader who doesn't dare
at this moment question who she is
and why she's up there? Father
stand you too far away too close? The words
of the hymn mean nothing see my mouth move as
your boyfriend whispers you a secret
and you smile. A green cord
spans the floor and snakes up
through the songleader's mike and if I tore it
with two sweating hands I'd
surely die and
you and she and all the living would
you smile? The globe drops
shaken from the pine: laughing you look at me I'm there
in your glasses: our tongues
move as hers moves, together: her eyes
closed her head nodding we can't
share the hymn she feels
in her throat. Even
being swallowed father could we?

Look at the Obese Loser Trying Not to Pray

to my dead brother

You faraway Holy
Ghost filling my skull don't You remember
the widow next door She failed to censor
off her drunken pool's scum breeding
mosquitoes Why did our mother and father try
evicting her? I could have
loved her We heard
from her shadowy kitchen sizzling
pork-smells Did she choke her body free in there Me
   stretched out flat
skull raped by soap-smells on the
laundry-room's hard carpet
the weak floor trembling at the washing-
machine's rumbling maybe all
she'd felt dissolved into her
home The dawn after
I'd shoved You off my treehouse breaking open Your
   head to free
her ghost I keep
evicting back through shadows we slunk
out to our private
burned-down chickencoop to scribble
on its charred puddles of rain her name *Christopher* in
piss Why did You
tell me she'll feel trapped until "death" takes me? Ben
I came home early from Your tear-stupid funeral I crept
back inside
our living-room's cold cave I
curled I twitched like a larva born on mental scum on its
lake-bottom deep blue and
in the carpet found a hole
where the vacuum-cleaner's pink seemingly
endless missing hose should fit I
opened the silver trap I prayed
You'd feel these wants like
any brother should You'd
switch on the groaning central system from our
basement You'd suck
my skull safe into this warm house make the

29

two of us one ghost Please let
my nerves be home's
"immutable" wires
A door slams Please
seem someone real at last Don't
let Ben take me

Any Nest I Can't Sleep in Should Be Burned

These chaste
words go out
to you, rough ogress Mrs. Hardcastle trying
like hell to get me axed maybe
you think you really
ought to be the best maybe
answering the phones I come off
smarter? Your imagination
is it *stripped clean*
of love
the way mine is? Why's your
son always so late
picking you up? The disorganized
red pens on your desk do tell
the future Who do you think keeps dis-
connecting your son's
calls Your crossed
arms like luscious hams safe
at your breasts why can't
you
keep aiming that
glare back into this full-length mirror called our body
    staring
down. Moving gently these bare
hands. Moaning *Let me*
in
this ton of air torn out
cold lungs
I can't be helped Your stare trans-
fixed out onto the wind-washed
parking-lot I feel there won't be
any future
known or
blank
unless You hold me

If We Can't Surrender Greed to Love We'll Murder Earth

in the Post Office

Atlas-muscled
mail-tray-heaving hunk-of-Life shielded

from me too behind
thick glass each time I blink I
snap off a leaf
from *your* world yet your heartbeat dares to
knit it back on
without my
input? Can't you hear it's almost *me* breathing out
loud not Fatso choking
his lungs filling with cold
chlorine-stinking water my chilling mother weeping *help*
   me sinking back
into these arms
Pathetic Fatso I guess *did* hear her sob
as the Arranging Mind failed
in their bed once more to
hold her He's a
snapshot of God my Flinching Father loosely taped
over my husband's
glass lenses? whose eyes keep failing
at each breakfast to be choked
by God's glare shot from His Heaven into the
shallow
black pools behind
these eyelids because
Fatso has to fail not
to let each damned bite gag him Each night I feel
at love's instant of freedom this body blaze
then having had myself at last still
fail to sleep O silent
postman try touching
me Seems like I'm sunk
into a world of ghosts
for nothing

Dying in Your Garden of Death to Go Back into My Garden

Toppled
down backward six feet through stifled heat
onto dry grass. The sacrificial
smell of grilling beef.
Telephone cables jammed with chit-chatting starlings
    make self-consciousness the sky. I
grind my spine in to know how hard I can
push toward You

without dying. God
You are this old globe Earth. Press
my cold bones back down into time's passing.
Tap Your deepest river with my spine,
my hindbrain's root. Turn
my brother's bones and my huge mother away from me.
Let me feel, in this silence of noon,
Your gold flesh.

From the jogging track's edge I kicked
a pigeon's torn-free wing into thick weeds.
Once You eat me
will You keep my flesh mute or fart wind?
The Jew next to me, sobbing
to feed his stabbed lungs air, his black-haired
torso golden with sweat,
turns his walkman up louder
—You won't
let me whisper through those headphones love's
dirge: goosestep

behind me, You mad
chattering God leaving this skull,

into the urine-scented
showers!

Easter

Sitting in this hospital waiting room
a fluorescent light humming like flies overhead
as outside the rain eats
at gunmetal-gray ice
while in a curtained room you get stitches
the human corpses meanwhile
pile up and pile up
in UPI photos and
I can think about it yes
even mention it but you
racing around the grumbling hood of a parked car
a loose tip of chrome siding knifed
your thigh through blue jeans
and you bled and
we hobbled here your arm around my shoulders and
    what if
you'd been brained on the ice
I would have gone on living but God tell me
when a man dies what changes
you killed my brother what can I do now
and if outside peace beckons
in the conscienceless rain
why can't I see it what's wrong and
please come out now I'll
help you walk home

34

Three

Clarence White Mumbling Goodbye

My friend we have if nothing else this moment between
   us
The rain pulled off your suit long ago that was nice
The corrosion took awhile Had you tried rebuilding
   your muscles it might not have
Then it ate up your flesh bones mind yes
perhaps even your soul Now that you've boarded
I must tell you I've watched closely the whole thing
It took no more than a moment Standing still
on two legs outside your bus in warm rain aren't we
one man My reflection
dissolving on wet silver lurches forward
Call to me I'll hold out tips where once hung arms

Clarence White Seeking Peace

Below me, next door, dwells a junkman. Isn't he God?
(Here, I've been reporting on him in this diary,
no one else. You may keep it.)
An old bloke, black, wrapped all the long day
and all night in a black bathrobe
brilliant with swirling silver fish
or are they stars? In his back yard,
set apart from the torn luggage, four television sets
I've heard him ask daytime clients not
to touch, all black-and-white
and all plugged in, surround
his worn-down-to-postureless gold armchair; all night
he sits sipping wine, drowned
in that set of sets' weightless blue solution
like a fetus, saying nothing, keeping their sound so low
he seems to hear them. Switching each set
randomly from broadcast to broadcast
without rising, he inspects
all at once the whole globe as it dissolves
in his breathless chuckling at reruns,
his lone sound. He's deep in dreams
by the time the static hits.
Soon I'll be wound in his bathrobe,
will I not? I shall keep my chuckling to myself.

Clarence White as Impotent God

Look, my teetering angel look
at him down there dancing with his eyes closed
as if strangled in swaddling clothes.
Isn't the heat of all the guys throbbing around him his
    partner?
When I opened those eyes
I could not tell whether it were poinsettia leaves or leaves
    of fire
encircling everyone's face: alone
trembling inside him I
clung that night to Hell: meekly
observing at this distance his clamped eyes, though, my
    voice seems
the drip-
drip of self-conscious blood onto marble.
The whole time he is dancing don't we sense he's evading
    some evil,
that there's a certain more deadly activity,
that a certain cloistered part of his body
must be raising its Godlike command? Must I
keep my mouth closed
my eyes shut? Fallen angel
can't I rub his warm planet on your face?

Clarence White's Lullaby

In a moist alley me alone wakeful propped upright
under a blanket of cold sunrise not you little leper
snuffling scratching coughing fast asleep

little pre-ghost turned hungrily away from me as if lice
    speak
and have learned to fear any society's urge to expand
and have requested we not share their fevered mattress

You now waking in shadow
of a bone-thin campanile your face dark
Twin blue heavens fading from your eyes Twin mirages
sucked back into dark sand

Not fade from here Hear me I'm a louse within your ear
hear me whisper tall tales in which your ear

If only my embrace could pull you back A
warm self-assertive machine gun fills my arms

Clarence White Exposed by High Noon

Can *you* see them back there
at the counter's far end, behind
this realm of cold dawn light
I can hardly see out from? Propped
at a dark hunch surely a table
there he is, the old man, and above
and behind him her profile,
trembling, gazing
down like a dark angel—between them, in the pale
   kitchen's light, cigarette smoke,
uncoiling from his ashtray, twining
with a snake of smoke
from her lips, rising
together,
disappearing.

Blushing away from them, down
into the carpet
could I have found
the green jungles of Champa, have seen
not that sequence of red ants
but an elephant caravan, each crumb
of doughnut a basket
filled—overflowing!—
with rough bread? I
blinked up and found
their gaze. Not far away now
in our little shop of shadows. Two
faces gashed
and bled dry, his hands rolling
the morning news into a tube, her eyes through
the stilled smoke trained
on a black insect feeling
down the blood-spackled wall toward
the coffee-machine, the old man's eyes *drinking*
me in, his first gripping
the weapon
as I lift this cup to my cold lips.

Progress

*In a daydream Clarence White finds himself in an upstairs
    office at the Museum of Natural History, New York City,
    1864. In a few minutes he will be interviewed by a group of
    politicians and scientists.*

Raised almost from birth by a family of pumas my
    snorting child-
hood before science kissed me seems far off
now as once a life alien to mine seemed
impossible Across the dry naked desert
from a sandstone ridge's crest I spotted
a cyclone of steam pacing west What personal
threat could it have posed
No more than a circling buzzard but I
scampered down into a cleft
Your hungry binoculars had seen me

No sir not yours In what cleft
hide you from this strange buzzard these boundaries
You're paid to bring me downstairs and
the ore of a coin kills its meaning The mapped air
hiding each of their ash-colored beards in still smoke
    they won't
lie next to me won't smell me
Yet you tell me they'll be more than half-interested

Before they told me
those scattered bones in the gorge below our den once
held erect my own mother and father I
happily crept on all fours
Too ungainly to hunt I robbed buzzard-nests
The sucked eggshells lay broken like skulls next to my
    head
They showed me arrows I
suspect I'll be asked to praise revenge

But these are my arms on these arm-rests
Already on cold nights
craving a rough tongue on my nape I crave

the last time I craved the craving
The tongue itself barely haunts me Unlike you
who according to that history
you lent me arrived here
chained to your brother in the hold of a ship
to feel my words die in feces and sweat
Please will you whom I don't know as yet repeat
all this downstairs

His Prayer

Listen midwife
we're both wedded to this Safeway's bakery section
otherwise we could enjoy our affair Feel

the cool sweating air the fluorescent
lights murmuring like flies
o doubtless it's summer in my fever I

lack thoughts almost completely The coagulated
sweet scent of doughnuts
their starry-glazed flesh-colored

flesh Behind the counter
our ash-haired mother in a baker's apron seemingly
slicing her apprentice's sweet fingers

into bitesized samples O
tell me does he hide angel's wings
under his clothes but below

us the dust fixating shoeprints to the desert-white
tiles like shapes of ghosts
as if I were a beaver and you

a misdirected Boy Scout since someone
faceless at this point (neither you nor I) trods before us
toward the counter wearing heavy-soled boots

and not Death but my angelic little brother if he nibbled

the stillborn summers you've pulled
out of my belly would he nibble himself and thus
starve or would I finally cease having to have them See

you've so helplessly revealed them
in neat rows here on this card table
little white loaves wrapped in plastic and I

44

crave that the dead return here the same way
you suck from me my breath through unfelt kisses
then disdain to take my corpse with you

my own head bowed toward the loaves now one more
    loaf
smothered in your breath's clear-plastic caul and
turned to stone

from which no water flows right here in front of
    everyone

Clarence White Reveals His True Identity

This morning I dreamed of a precocious lad
from the California suburbs; he was feebly
trying to grow muttonchop whiskers
having dyed his hair gray. He bore
his tombstone on his tongue.
He didn't prefer the little tablet,
he told me: it weighed less
than a feather and his friends
had learned his name from it
then had simply waddled away.
He felt, he said, as if he'd died
in several wars. I told him I'd truly seen elephants
lumbering off through the brush
toward their graveyard. Thank you,
he said, but only when the word
is made flesh we'll be happy. Trying
to conceal the bitter pill
under his watch's cold face, an act
he knew would shatter glass,
he bit through to his wrist.
What could I do? The blood
as it dried on his face made each whisker
love its neighbor. He lay
his head on his pillow,
his eyes closed. I
awoke.

The Film That Won't Stop,
That Has No Audience

Flying here, I said, I was sure
the plane would crash. I daydreamed
I walked through the fuselage walls and
sat down in this car, right here, with you
driving. You said, You're on vacation
and routine is important. Remember

last Christmas, I'd just moved to Hollywood
and was still scared your mother would find me?
I had to make new friends, find
the post office, learn the new streets
—I felt like a lost kid. I doubted
myself. Now, every night I

go dancing. My friends don't know me,
really, which is fine. I don't mind
being lost. Not inside, though. Did
you know I died once? Remember
that year you came down for her
birthday, and I had appendicitis?
She thought I'd done it on purpose?

Yeah? On the operating table—and they
told me I really was dead—I
was suddenly floating above it all
looking down at the surgeon, my
body, the incision. Then it was white,

that's all I saw, and I was
calm, I knew I was dead and
I was happy. It was good. Then I
felt his hands on me, reeling me in,
and that machine pounding my heart
into action. I didn't want to be alive.

I'm glad they brought you back
anyway, Dad. Oh yes. Now Alan
is Mina's second husband, a nice man—

I'm glad for her—her first,
you know, made B-movies. What's that?

I asked him later in their living room.
Alan clinked crystal in the kitchen. Sketches,
I guess, for his movie, *The Beast
of Hollow Mountain*. See, the beast was
animation, like in those silly Japanese films

but the cowboys and stagecoaches were real.
I said, It looks like a *Tyrannosaurus rex*.
Is that a cow it's lifting to its
mouth? I guess so, he said. Stand here. See
the ocean? Out that canyon's mouth. There's
Catalina. Remember? She took you there once.

In This Blackout

Our lad, turned
around in the back seat, pressing his knees
around the central hump in the floor, pressing
his nose down into
the cool blind chasm in the leather
as I told him to
(because his father's bladelike hands
were soon to fly from the wheel as I'd foreseen and snip
off his mother's head) though
shining brilliant on its shining
gray fur, was
gratefully no more than the day's heat
along the steel-cable nape of a wolfhound seen sniffing
down a path never ending
deep at the heart of one soft cell. A
thousand alcoholic-red roses edged this path
and lost no petals, though like the face of his mother
    they accused me
of kidnapping him. Does
he not see I've always
craved
his body? The wetness
at the beast's huge snout bled
from inside it
but when next I peered into my daydream, that pair of
    garden-shears driving
hadn't budged: snipped loose
I became our lad's werewolf, stalking
back down his optic nerve stem o Lord toward Your
    warm day never
suspecting I had stabbed
red blossoms in these sockets. I can't
part these eyelids? Is he sleeping
or dead?

Divorced Woman Nearing the Foothills—Ramona Expressway

for my mother

You want him. You want it to hurt
much worse, the boarded schoolhouse
severed from your shoulder
by hot glass, hot space
and what you know. You want
it to hurt the way heat must hurt
not feathers on the wings of the crows
but beige stucco walls stuck
in beige cooking dirt.
Tumbleweed loosed down the road:
empty skull. In the years
since you last passed here, no glass
put back in the windows: look in
past no-reflection, your ghost
in old raiments still prods
with a stick a dead pigeon laid out
like tragic on the assembly-hall stage
whilst, through twilit dust motes, the sound
of him peeing
in the corner still nudging
through your brain. Crows
outside car know all about the mute
dump, make circles
in a desert of sky, caw nothing
and *that* points the way

to where you're going:
the mountains where evergreens suck at snowy earth
and where, in a patch of melting snow,
you saw a bitch bark, watching over
your kids on a bobsled. House
that should have been a wigwam:
smell of pines, in an ant's jaws
a beige petrified cookie crumb,
smell of everything you're not

we must map from on high.

Clarence White's Angel Is a Witch

At this point she spends her whole day slumped over,
asleep, her breath
wordless, lost
somewhere above the clouds.
A hint I should likewise relax? Such an effort
exhausts me—breathing
deeply I can't help thinking
of heaven, that plastic bag over my head.
In her sleep she chuckles monstrously:
talking somewhere with someone I can't see
is to her taste.
The food she demanded I cook
she refuses: I can't predict
which aromas will pierce her
nor what she'll scoff at or sample once awake.
If I could only forget I'm her host!
"Eat so that I may eat," I ask aloud
—her snore thrusts
me back into the gnawing
dilemma of Will vs. Infancy.
She called it that, I think.
In all this I'm not different from you.
Of course she won't let me love another.

Heaven on Earth! Unlike her
I come from somewhere—a house in the country,
you've seen them. Yesterday
you rapped at my door and I was glad
you woke me. She slept
—but had I dreamed her growling
in my ear? I
should have let you in anyway.
In half an hour of quiet talk
could we have saved each other's mortal souls?
Regret pulls
her breath through my ears
and through my nostrils,
and here at my own table
I'm her dream.   51

Clarence White Escapes His Demon Lover

My belly pressed to earth's grassy belly only *my* belly
    growling
So Afterlife you perpetual hunger you must be here too
I had hoped behind these bushes I might get some

A man-sized rook in a Zulu warmask coming at me
swollen-chested bearing through an army of sparrows a
    Charles Atlas gym bag
he's shiny he's black in his dust-stinking feathers he's
    enslaved me

No one's out there Try it Clarence Okay I'm writhing out
    of my shirt
Will he fill me like a nuclear whiteout blooming in a
    rearview mirror I'd give
anything Should I turn over He's lord of earth and earth
    itself I can't believe he'd be attracted to my flab

On the trampled spear grass on either side of my beak-
    clenched head the grounded tips of his wings I can't
    look He wants to smother me in grass
his growling belly pressing down on my spine The
    stench of grass jabbing up into my head punches in
    the floor of our chapel a hole
and leaves it gaping for the warm marble bone of his
    bird-hips to push in through

If in fact he's a man why should he seem light as a
    feather He's pounding me into his hips pounding in
    mine and from somewhere
under my hips tugging me down
through moaning grass into earth's dungeon O bury
    Clarence Satan have yourself

Clarence White Meets Father Christmas

Behind her the Pussycat Theater, its wide doorway
motherly and moaning. Her glass prism glowing
in my eyes, a spool of tickets
at her elbow like Saint Peter, should I ask her
what's brought her here to float
inside the heat, her
face wrinkled as if pickled
in her own ash-cloud breath? Sunset
has sucked sweat from her armpits, spit it out
in half-moons under her sleeves
—mathematics, however, seem simplistic: I crawl toward her
in a Salvation Army-issue Santa suit, palms down
on the parched sidewalk, rubbing
gently her sore back where at the same time my hand
    straying
to my lap I sit here in this cool
dark viewing room watching her
watching me watch her through the eye
of a camera aimed down at her waiting for the moment
    her hand strays
south to bury an old page
under its just-used younger brother in the yellowing
novel on her lap. She puffs
she puffs her cigarette She's seen me She's
trying to smokescreen her face. If she'd promise
to make me into pure fable I would give her
completely to her body: in twelve minutes
a Chevrolet now veering from the freeway swerves
drunkenly wide in its left turn—its front left fender breaks
my knees, my skull splintered
by its back leftside tire. At that moment
let my whole life flash
like sunbeam in her eyes—*in*
her eyes, as we say, not *before* them—her eyes
closed tightly against gore-splattered glass—let her enter
the theater forever dark
and moist
a safe baby dear father
in Your tomb   53

Song about a Meadow in Sunset

My mother imagines I don't want my fast car
apparently. Is *that* what she thinks?
How dare she dream I even dream of it
here, glinting brilliantly elsewhere so shyly? The genius
    of silver, it must in heaven
command the sun's whole lap
—it's so bright these mortal eyes can never taint it.
Not death, but a vision of death without dying, it's a
gift to me from God my Deathless Father, but should it
blast through this meadow of hers one would glimpse it
    reduced,
merely her sun on her seasonal orbit and it would
    instantly
leave behind itself desert
and my ash.

                    Mother
to try describing its upholstery would wound you, our
    eye would see only your bloodstains
If it's merely some me inside some mirror craving me it's
    my hearse
here O father
can I wait past Easter again for it?
And then as usual past Christmas? Your chill breath
in these veins chills her blood, these knees
in her soft, green hair feel too brittle and
she wants you, she forces me always to address you
as if you've ever had ears, as if
this mouth weren't frozen shut, as if I've ever been more
    than
something moaning along with her teen-hymns
in this brain, something drowning her out, steering

toward you more quickly than light while
kneeling pinkly so soft in her red sunset,
these parallel arms lifted slightly

54

the stink of rosemary sucking you out through these
    nostrils
a dead evergreen wreath falls from these hands I can't
    see
my ghost climb trembling to your lap as you
press this ear forever hers into her dust

Fifty-two Lines of Iambic Pentameter

The books are lying on the floor in dis-
array. The phone is blue like sky is blue.
Talking to Claudia, we talk about
the works of Ezra Pound and Henry James:
she wants to write a paper on the sense
of time in Ezra Pound. She says that when
she's sixty, she'll be floating off the ground
six feet. I say I only want to kiss
and never stop. It's almost eight o'clock;
it's Sunday; it's a dense and snowy night.
But Claudia is at the laundromat
and now her clothes are dry, so she hangs up.
And I go back to writing, though it's not
as if I stopped, despite the gruesome pain,
losing oneself in darkened, pathless woods,
etcetera, which may be just repression.
Now Steve is talking on the phone, smoking.
He slaps his knee—does this mean that he's glad
to be alive, or not? He's laughing now,
that's good; he's talking to a friend of his
who teaches up in Michigan, whose name
is Mary-Lou. They're talking about Dads,
about how mine is "coming out." Of what?
It's just a way of saying it—why be
a jerk about what's said and isn't said
and how? In physics now, the world is all
connected up in "Patterns of Organ-
ic Energy," which I don't understand
as yet, but will . . . oh, what I'm getting at:
the "it" that we find other ways of saying,
if it were everything, the world, what would
it matter how we spoke of anything?
Maybe it's good to have just one of this
and something absolutely else of that
and the right word for each of these to help
us keep them separated in our minds—
which after all is where it counts, our eyes
becoming blinded by TV and soot.
I frankly think it's harder done than said—

take Ezra Pound, for instance, though perhaps
this isn't fair. Now Steve's twisting the cord
on the blue phone, that cord which is a rope
dropped down from heaven so that he may talk
with Mary-Lou in Michigan, eons
away, or almost, on a snowy night
in January, which is ending now.
I like these iambs, actually: they help
one talk about dull stuff musically;
they also do help make things black and white
and logical, though Claudia is on
her way home through the snow, her clothes
clean now, and on her head like Africa.

Clarence White Seduced by an Icecube

Little skull I would fish you from this sweat-
and-precipitation-beaded seltzer-tumbler pressed
to my forehead and transport
you down the Embassy steps into the jungle all around
    us

in a hot clearing place you in an orchid's mouth to watch
you crack hear fissures crack through you like raw
    impulse and crack
you I would punch your card in at the time-clock

smell the blush on the petals of the orchid's
deaf use of your zero-meaning whisper Dip
my finger in the liquor of your death

seal my own lips with that finger taste
your chill blood taste it well and with you fade
not into heaven but the fly-filled
warm air I have failed

here to nurture independence doling
out money to the pygmies and by your bleeding you
    should be feeding plants We're both torn
from the impotent north and still homesick

apparently melting now into ourselves not to die
every thought a defeat in swollen bodies so strange
they seem familiar pulled
helplessly by tides and held in glass

Clarence White's Prom Night

Isn't there some place
you and I could sneak off to
to be without him for a time,
a long time? You,
reader, the true you, with whom I share the name
    Clarence, your puckered
lips blossom
alien to *his* ear.

Bite,
won't you, since
this all will
pop soon, that absurd
red rose from his lapel

—no let him alone let him build me
into a
church you too may lose
your death in, lost
forever, clutching your own skull and
(since he won't
rescue anyone's body) calling it mine—me tongueing
for a last time
the Spring's sweet hash
into your ear?

The Sacrifices

The Sacrifices

As a child I read books on advances
in the science of human anatomy made,
unfortunately, perhaps unavoidably, during the Civil
  War.
Taking my instructions from the latest issue of *Modern
  Science*,
in order to know life and assuming
such knowledge would finally
after a long life of failures and impotencies warm my
  heart to it, I cut
a rectangle of surface flesh
from a cow's side,
just below the ribs, and installed a window there, not of
  glass
but of a flexible, heat-retaining plastic.
The drugged cow had no complaints. It thrilled me
after sponging away the blood
to sort out and identify the various muscles,
tubes and arteries I found there. Having located
its large and small intestines, I
fed the animal bright things . . . orange sherbet—
to watch the diluted orange juices
flow through the transparent tubes, and my mind no less
  active
than the enzymes churning in the stomach. I myself
would sometimes eat sherbet by the bowlful
until its sugar and chemicals did their work
on my bloodstream, on my mind.
Like a friendly, excitable tick-bird I'd jump up and down
around the brute, kiss it
daintily around the ears, search its bristly hair for
  insects.
Meanwhile the dumb thing munched on and on, eating
  carrots,
mangoes, a bright coin even, and finally
chomping thoughtlessly at a beam of thin sunlight
entering the barn through a high, lone window.
This gave me pause. The cow gradually
grew silent, lost interest

in masticating solid foods.
I'd done irreparable damage. Its eyes
which had held so gently its world of hay and droppings
had the near-sighted stare of fish-eyes.
I found a ladder, climbed
to the window and, risking my life,
managed to nail over it a canvas sheet.
It was too late. I started drinking as I never had—not
    even as a student—before.
Around two or two-thirty one morning, upon finishing
my fifth or sixth fifth,
Poor friend, I said to it, Perversion,
though a man's stock in trade, is terrible to impose on a
    poor brute
such as yourself. Now
all I wish for you is freedom
from this nudity, a good romp in the fields,
a handsome bull, and that pleasure you've lost—yes,
I know you've lost it, the sedatives long ago wore off—in
    the sound
of your own voice, your own inarticulate groanings, that
    lovesong
to your undoubted self. What am I
to punish you? What narcissism
led me to such butchery? Was it revenge?
Against whom? I flung
my bottle into the hay,
undoubtedly crushing some field mouse, stripped off
my own clothes, stood pathetically
in front of the beast, half-blind still
from gazing up that Yellow Brick Road.
Its sweet breath tickling my leg-hairs
I stood there naked
before it. Do you see,
my friend, as I can't hope to see, what truly I am?
Can I do more than this? That question
haunted me and hurt me. At night
I couldn't shut my eyes
—whenever I did its brown eyes, its wifely eyes

would close in on me, look at me. Nor
could I go out to buy more bourbon,
dressed as I wasn't and afraid
to observe that lack of shame I'd always, it seems to me
    now,
seen my reasonable peers wear so well.
At last I buried myself
in the moist hay, to the unexposed side
of my friend, knowing
it would smell me. And so hate me.
Hoping it would not hate remembrance. My plan
is that one hungry morning it will turn on its rope
seeking a new patch of fodder
and find my innocent hand,
perhaps a foot. I
lie here, lost to myself, knowing nothing, scenting
    nothing
but hay rot and an occasional fresh load of shit, hearing
    nothing but
that slow, constant chewing
and now and then a thud
signaling a nap,
its spine toward me, I imagine.
I wait, then it
rises to its hooves,
those muted hooves, and I hear it
shaking its thick hide. I imagine hay fragments
jettisoned through air. Thank God I never thought
to bell its neck. Awhile ago
just as a field mouse started nibbling
at my toe, one of the nuns living nearby—planting
wheat, sickling wheat, tending the barn—came in
as usual to pet my raped friend
and ask it her dolorous, habitual why
her pained why. Poor girl
she's looking for answers, chains of cause,
a place for shame in some discernible plan.
On good mornings I'm dulled
to her anguish, can't share it, and so

am able to lie:
I tell myself all this, my whole life,
is for her own good, her career.
A young woman kneeling
in a barn. Only she
can never know whom it is she now must love,
a sneeze from the hay would damn her.
The frightened mouse scampered away. It will
come back with its friends, who doubtless also pray
    hungrily.